EDWIN LUCAS

St. Clare of Assisi

Her Biography, Novena, and Prayers in Honor of the Patron Saint of Eye Diseases, the Poor, and Purity

Contents

Introduction

Welcome to the "St. Clare of Assisi," a sacred and soul-enriching journey that will lead you into the radiant world of one of the most beloved saints in Christian history – St. Clare of Assisi. Within these pages, you will discover a tapestry of spirituality, miracles, and prayers that have touched the hearts of countless faithful over the centuries.

As the author of this book, I am humbled to guide you through the life, teachings, and intercession of St. Clare, a remarkable woman whose devotion to God has left an indelible mark on the world. My personal encounter with the profound devotion to St. Clare inspired me to create this book, where I hope to share the extraordinary grace and blessings that have been bestowed upon those who turn to her in prayer.

The feast day of St. Clare, celebrated on August 11th, marks a time of special reverence and devotion among those who have experienced her powerful intercession. In this book, we will journey through the life of St. Clare, from her early days of privilege to her radical decision to follow the path of poverty, contemplation, and service to God.

Through intimate anecdotes and historical insights, I invite you to walk alongside St. Clare as she encounters St. Francis of Assisi, a meeting that would forever change her life. Witness the unfolding of their spiritual friendship and how it led to the establishment of the Order of Poor Clares, a community devoted to a life of simplicity, prayer, and selfless service.

Within these sacred pages, you will find the powerful novena prayers composed in honor of St. Clare. These prayers have been a source of comfort and strength for generations of faithful souls seeking solace, healing, and hope. Each day of the novena holds a unique opportunity for you to connect with St. Clare, allowing her to intercede on your behalf before God.

Meet St. Clare the person, not just St. Clare the saint. Gain a good understanding of St. Clare's life and times and why she is such a revered saint.

Biography of St. Clare

The Ancestry of Clare

C lare's noble lineage can be traced back to her paternal great-grandfather, Paolo, who belonged to the esteemed Counts of Scefi family, owning citadels and palaces in and around Assisi. Her grandfather, Offreduccio, the sole child in his family, possessed a grand house situated in the upscale and fashionable Piazza San Ruffino. Offreduccio had three sons, and one of them, Favarone, would become Clare's father.

Favarone, a wealthy knight, presided over a highly esteemed household, employing numerous servants and being a prominent figure throughout the district. Clare's mother, Ortolana, held the title of Countess of Sterpeto and was deeply beloved by the people of Assisi for her charitable acts and devout religious lifestyle. Despite the challenges and risks involved in traveling during that time, Ortolana embarked on numerous pilgrimages, including journeys to Rome and even as far as Jerusalem in the Holy Land itself. The name "Ortolana" in Italian translates to "gardener," and fittingly, as a mother, she played a pivotal role in nurturing her daughter's faith.

1

Favarone and Ortolana were blessed with five children. Unfortunately, their firstborn, Bosone, a boy and the heir, passed away prematurely. The remaining children were Penenda, the eldest daughter, followed by Agnes, whose baptismal name was Catherine, and Beatrice, the third and fourth daughters. Yet, our focus now turns to the second and most exceptional daughter, Clare.

From Birth to Maidenhood

In the Middle Ages, childbirth was a daunting experience, and as Ortolana's child's arrival neared in 1193, she found solace in prayer at the Basilica of San Ruffino. Kneeling before the crucifix, she fervently prayed for a safe delivery and a smooth childbirth. In her prayers, she heard a reassuring voice saying, "Do not be afraid... for you will safely give birth to a light whose rays shall illuminate the whole world." And so, on July 16th, 1193, Clare entered the world, her eyes seeing the sun for the very first time.

When it came time to baptize the child, Ortolana recalled God's comforting words and named her Chiara, Clare, which means "light" or "to illuminate." It was a hope that this brightness would somehow fulfill God's divine promises. As a mother, Ortolana diligently brought up Clare, teaching her the ways of faith and guiding her in prayer. Ortolana's own pious life served as a perfect example for her young daughter to follow. Additionally, Clare's devout widow aunt, Bona Guelfuccio, became her governess and confidante, offering encouragement and support while gaining deep insight into Clare's true spiritual nature.

Assisi had its share of poverty-stricken areas, with many

struggling to survive in dismal conditions. Even as a young girl, Clare displayed signs of her sanctity by secretly sacrificing her own delicacies from household meals and sharing them with the poor and orphaned, aided by one of her aunt's daughters. Prayer became an integral part of Clare's life, often spending hours hidden away in the rooms of her home, conversing with God. Lacking a set of prayer beads, she would use tiny pebbles to count her "Our Fathers" and direct her heartfelt prayers to the Lord. Immersed in Divine Love, Clare began to detach herself from worldly possessions, considering them as worthless. Underneath her outwardly normal appearance, she wore a hair shirt, a symbol of her devotion to Christ.

Towards the end of the twelfth century, there was an uprising, causing many noble families, including Clare's, to seek refuge in the rival city of Perugia. In this new city, Clare forged lasting friendships with two girls, Filippa and Benvenuta, who would later be among the first to follow Clare's religious path. After three years, the war between Assisi and Perugia ended, and Clare returned to her beloved Assisi.

At the age of seventeen, Clare had blossomed into a woman of great beauty. Her family was respected and wealthy, and her father had grand plans for her marriage, seeking a suitor of noble and admirable virtues. There was no shortage of prospective suitors, but Clare adamantly refused any notion of marriage. Despite her father's annoyance and insistence, Clare stood firm in her desire to remain chaste and dedicate her virginity to the Lord.

Clare, Francis, and the Divine Calling

Assisi had already embraced St. Rufinus as its patron saint, but the city was soon to witness the extraordinary presence of not just one but two of the Church's greatest saints. Born in 1182, Francis Bernardone, senior to Clare by eleven years, hailed from a well-known family with his father being one of the city's wealthiest merchants. In his youth, Francis reveled in social gatherings and dreamt of becoming a great knight.

However, a life-altering experience awaited him when he embarked on an adventurous journey southwards dressed in extravagant armor, only to return changed and different within a few days. From that moment, a calling from God compelled him to renounce worldly possessions, live in poverty, and dedicate himself wholly to God. This marked Francis' conversion, and he prophesized the future arrival of a community of "Poor Ladies."

News of Francis' eccentric behavior spread throughout Assisi as he and his disciples begged for sustenance. While some viewed him as a madman, others recognized true holiness in his actions, and young Clare would have undoubtedly heard of this intriguing and faithful servant of God.

In 1209, Francis' Order of Friars Minor received verbal approval from Pope Innocent III, and he began preaching, emphasizing the importance of poverty in gaining everything in God. Inspired by this radical way of life, Clare sought out Francis, whose new order became her spiritual guide and father in faith.

Clare's conversion was not tied to a specific moment; it seemed predestined from her mother's womb. Upon her return from Perugia, Clare devoted herself to assisting the poor, offering prayers, and practicing penance for the love of Jesus. She withdrew from the outside world, making her rooms a secluded cloister and her life of prayerful solitude began.

As Clare's devotion and piety became known throughout Assisi, her fame for holiness reached Francis himself. Eager to see and hear him, Clare frequently visited Francis, accompanied by her trusted Aunt Bona Guelfuccio or faithful friends. Francis revealed to her the emptiness of worldly pursuits and urged her to consecrate her body and soul solely to God.

Over the next two years, Francis guided Clare to new spiritual heights, instilling fervent love for Jesus in her heart. He encouraged her to desire nothing but Christ, to seek only the Creator, Redeemer, and Savior. Clare embraced poverty as the path to eternal joy, aching to become a bride of the heavenly King.

Following Francis' lead, Clare chose to renounce her privileged life and embrace poverty as her path. Now, the challenge was to discern a way to fulfill God's divine plan for her.

Clare's Flight From Home

Clare sought Francis' guidance to fulfill her divine calling, and with the approval and counsel of Bishop Guido of Assisi, a plan was set in motion. On the day before Palm Sunday in 1212, a tense strategy was carefully orchestrated to remove Clare from the world's burdens. As the Lenten twilight gave way to darkness, Clare put her plan into action.

With miraculous strength, Clare and her cousin Pacifica overcame obstacles to sneak out of the house unnoticed. Under the moonlight's guidance, they ventured to the Church of St. Mary of the Porziuncula, where Francis and his followers awaited, keeping a night vigil with torches ablaze. There, Clare underwent the symbolic tonsure and took on the humble garb of a habit, establishing the threefold Franciscan Order.

Upon discovering Clare's absence, her family grieved and condemned her decision. They pleaded with her to return, resorting even to verbal abuse and threats, but Clare remained steadfast in her devotion to Christ. In an act of defiance, she publicly removed her veil, revealing her shaved head, and making it clear that nothing would sway her from her path.

Seeking safety, Clare transferred to the Benedictine monastery of San Angelo di Pansa on the slopes of Mount Subasio. Only a short time later, another dramatic event occurred when Clare's sister, Agnes, decided to follow in her footsteps. Clare had been praying for this, and Agnes' arrival was anticipated. However, their father, Favarone, driven by anger, led a group to forcibly bring Agnes back home.

The party cunningly gained access to the convent and, faced with Agnes' refusal, resorted to violence. They brutally assaulted Agnes, but Clare knelt in prayer, beseeching God for her sister's release. An astonishing miracle occurred, making Agnes too heavy to be carried further. Eventually, Clare convinced the assailants to leave her half-dead sister in her care.

Agnes became the first follower of Clare's soon-to-be-founded community, as they established their humble dwelling not far from the church Francis had restored with his own hands. The bond between the two sisters united in faith and their commitment to God's destiny, would set the foundation for Clare's future religious community.

A Life of Contemplation and Enclosure

Located just outside the eastern wall of Assisi, the Church, and monastery of San Damiano became Clare's sacred abode in 1212, upon the advice of Francis. Having already given her dowry to the poor at San Angelo, Clare embraced the simplicity and poverty of this humble dwelling, where she would spend the next forty-two years of her life. Within the confines of her small cell, cloisters, garden, and chapel, Clare withdrew from the outside world, immersing herself in self-imposed solitude. This heavenly nest on earth became her sanctuary of silence, prayer, penance, and poverty, as she wholeheartedly dedicated herself to charity and caring for those who chose to follow this rigorous form of religious life. Her ultimate mission was to pray and bring souls closer to her beloved Lord. Initially known as the "Poor Ladies" of the Order of San Damiano (The Damianites), Clare's unique order gained recognition.

Clare's sanctity and fame quickly spread throughout the region, and the community of two (Clare and her sister Agnes) began to grow. Soon after, two of Clare's close childhood friends, Benvenuta from Perugia and Pacifica, joined. Inspired by Clare's holiness, many rich young maidens willingly gave up their possessions to follow Christ's path under her guidance. Mothers encouraged their daughters, and daughters encouraged their mothers to join the monastery. Sisters followed in their sisters' footsteps, and nieces and aunts also sought to dedicate their lives to Christ within the enclosure. Beyond the monastery's walls, attitudes began to change, and more men joined Francis' First Order of Brothers. Married couples also explored ways of adopting a simplified way of life at home, unbound by monastic rules. This was an early form of what would later become the Third Franciscan Order (The Tertiary) for the laity. Although secluded, Clare was now fulfilling the prophecy, illuminating the world from within.

As many young girls and women underwent conversion, Clare sent out her sisters to establish new convents and monasteries in Italy and neighboring countries. In her lifetime, Clare witnessed the founding of around one hundred and fifty houses of her Order. More and more individuals willingly embraced this way of life, answering the call to live simply and, more importantly, to live according to the Gospel.

The Privileges of Poverty

After three years of devoted religious life, Clare remained steadfast in her desire to be a humble servant sister, serving Christ and her fellow sisters with unwavering humility. She had no ambitions for authority or titles, but in obedience to Francis, whom the sisters affectionately called their "holy father," and the local Bishop, Clare reluctantly accepted the position of Abbess, a role she would hold until her death.

Despite her new responsibilities, Clare never shied away from any task. She would humbly wash the hands of her sisters, serve meals, and wait on them at the table. Instead of giving orders, she preferred to take on extra work herself, exemplifying the virtue of humility. Her compassion knew no bounds; she cared for sick sisters, washing their bodies and soiled clothing without hesitation or repulsion. When a lay sister arrived at the monastery, Clare would immediately kneel and clean and dry their feet as a gesture of humble service.

Living the Gospel meant living without any material possessions. The community rejected all worldly goods and relied solely on the work of their own hands. This new women's Order, known as the "Poor Ladies," followed a set of rules written down by Francis in 1215, centered on doing penance, living according to the Gospel, practicing Christian love, and remaining faithful to the Catholic Church. Among these ideals, it was Clare's emphasis on compassion and poverty that left a lasting impact.

In 1215, Clare approached Pope Innocent III with a unique request. She wanted her order to bear the name "Poor" and sought "The Privilege of Poverty," affirming their complete renunciation of possessions. The Pope was astonished by Clare's fervor and granted her request, making history as no such privilege had ever been requested before. Despite later attempts by Pope Gregory IX to persuade Clare to accept possessions, she firmly held to her ideals, and "The Privilege of Poverty" was confirmed.

Clare renewed her vows to follow Christ alone, finding joy in receiving small morsels of bread that the lay Franciscan brothers begged for them, rather than a whole loaf. This practice epitomized her understanding of poverty and brought her profound contentment.

Bread and Oil Miracles

In the early days of the Poor Ladies' formation, Francis and his Order took on the responsibility of tending to their spiritual needs, always offering assistance whenever required. Though Francis visited occasionally, he had appointed a chaplain, a priest, and two lay brothers called Questors to cater to the sisters' needs. These lay brothers' main duty was to collect alms for the Poor Ladies, and there was a small hospice near the San

Damiano monastery, where a group of Friars resided. These Friars would beg for food to sustain the sisters' physical needs.

One day, an unusual occurrence arose when there was only one single loaf of bread left in the monastery. As mealtime approached, the sisters, who were already hungrier than usual, gathered in the refectory. Clare, the holy Abbess, instructed the sister in charge of the kitchen to divide the loaf in half: one half for the Friars and the other half to be shared among the sisters. Clare then requested the sister to cut fifty slices from the remaining half of the loaf and serve them on the table. The sister expressed her doubts, believing a special miracle from Christ would be needed to multiply that small piece of bread into fifty portions. Unfazed, Clare encouraged her, saying, "Do what I say and trust in me." The sister hurriedly complied with the request. Meanwhile, Mother Clare humbly prayed to Jesus, her beloved Spouse, on behalf of her fellow sisters. To everyone's amazement, as the sister began cutting the bread, it multiplied miraculously through divine intervention, providing more than enough for the entire community to eat.

Similarly, on another occasion, the supply of olive oil used for preparing food had completely run out. This oil, known for its health benefits, was typically given to sick sisters. Clare took an earthenware oil jar, washed and dried it by hand, and then placed the empty vessel outside the monastery's gate for the Lay Brother to take on his errand to obtain more oil. The devoted Lay Brother, eager to help with their needs, quickly noticed the single vessel lying on the wall in the shade and rushed to fetch it. Once again, through Clare's prayers, God filled the jar with oil, rendering the Brother's services unnecessary on that particular day. Initially, the brother suspected that the sisters were playing a trick on him, but upon realizing what had happened, he exclaimed joyfully that "the jar was full."

As time passed, the Order's ranks expanded widely, and by 1219, Clare had sent her own sister Agnes, with the title of Abbess, to oversee the monastery of Monticello near Florence. More and more mature ladies, widows, and princesses from other nations found solace in the sanctuaries of the Lord, leading to the foundation of the "Damianites" at Rheims in France and Spain by the late 1220s. Even Clare's mother, Ortolana, after becoming a widow, sold all her possessions and joined San Damiano, clothed in the habit by Francis himself. Following in her sister's footsteps, Clare's sister Beatrice took her vows with the "new family" at the age of eighteen and, under Clare's guidance, established several new monasteries throughout Italy.

Instances of Francis and His Relationship with Clare

Shortly after Francis had given Clare and the "Order of Poor Ladies" his simple Rule, he turned to Clare for guidance in humility concerning his own ministry. Feeling drawn to the contemplative life, Francis had been living as a hermit for some time. Though Clare considered herself unworthy of advising him, she sought God's answer through prayer, which led her to tell Francis to give up his solitude and continue proclaiming the Gospel. Clare rarely left San Damiano during her forty-two years there, but she made an exception when Francis invited her, at her insistence, to share a simple meal and "break bread" with him. Accompanied by a sister from the convent, Clare joined Francis for the meal at St. Mary of the Angels, the small Church known as The Porziuncula, located at the foot of Assisi, where she had received her humble habit years ago.

During the meal, Francis, Clare, and their companions were so immersed in a heavenly ecstasy that the locals outside perceived a great fire illuminating the night sky, seemingly rising from within the church. In response, the people of Assisi rushed to the scene with water to save the church, woods, and olive trees from destruction, only to find that the glowing light emanated from a "Divine Fire" fueled by the flames of "Divine love" in the dinner party. In 1224, Francis received the Holy Stigmata—the five wounds of the crucified Lord in his hands, feet, and side. For two years, Clare tenderly cared for him, attending to his intense sufferings by bandaging his wounds, wiping away the blood, and crafting sandals for his feet that bore the painful marks of the nails. During this time, Francis sensed that "Sister bodily death" was calling him, and he expressed his desire to be near the Church of San Damiano, which he himself had built, and to be in the presence of Clare and the sisters.

For the remainder of his days, Francis resided in a small hut made of mud and straw within the precincts of the monastery. It was during this period that Clare began experiencing her own bodily pains and infirmities, which persisted until the end of her life. Amidst these circumstances, Francis composed not only his famous "Canticle of the Sun," a beautiful hymn celebrating creation and nature, but also another song dedicated to his beloved sisters.

The Hymn of Divine Creation

O Most High, omnipotent, benevolent Lord,
All praise, glory, honor, and blessings are Yours alone.
Your Name, Most High, belongs exclusively to You, and mortal tongues cannot adequately utter it.

Praised be You, my Lord, alongside all Your creations,
especially Brother Sun, the source of light in our day.
His brilliance reflects Your grandeur, O Most High.
Praised be You, my Lord, through Sister Moon and the stars,
bright and beautiful, adorning the heavens.
Praised be You, my Lord, through Brothers Wind and Air,
gentle and turbulent, caring for all Your creations.
Praised be You, my Lord, through Sister Water, humble, pure,
and essential for life.
Praised be You, my Lord, through Brother Fire, illuminating
the night with its playful and powerful presence.
Praised be You, my Lord, through our Sister, Mother Earth,
nurturing and governing us, providing abundant fruits,
flowers, and herbs.
Blessed are those who forgive in Your name and endure trials
with love for You, for they shall be rewarded by You, Most
High.
Praised be You, my Lord, through Sister Death, inevitable for
all living beings. Woe to those who depart in sin, but blessed
are those who follow Your Will.
For them, no harm can come from the second death. I praise
and bless my Lord, offer thanks, and humbly serve Him.

The Song Saint Francis Wrote for The Poor Clare

Hear, dear Little Poor Ladies, called by the Lord's embrace,
Gathered from distant lands in unity and grace;
Devote yourselves to love and loyal care,
In obedience, find peace, and surrender all despair.

Turn not to worldly things, but seek the Spirit's way,
    In the life of holiness, you'll find a brighter day;
    With wisdom, use the gifts God's providence bestows,
    For your needs and for others, let love in action flow.

In sickness and in health, endure with steadfast heart,
    Such burdens carry blessings, a sacred, noble part;
    For each of you, a crown awaits in heaven's embrace,
    Queens with the Virgin Mary, in God's eternal grace.

As Francis' days drew close, within the Porziuncula's walls,
    He penned these words of guidance, before his final calls.

St. Francis' Last Will Written for Clare and Her Sisters

"I, Brother Francis, am devoted to following the life of poverty exemplified by our Lord Jesus Christ and His Most Holy Mother. My commitment to this path is unwavering, and I intend to persevere until the end. My dear ladies, I beseech and advise you always to embrace this sacred way of life and poverty. Be vigilant and protect yourselves diligently, lest you stray from this path due to the teachings or advice of others." ·

On October 3rd, 1226, an hour after sunset, Francis passed away. Clare had one final request of Francis, to see him one last time. Her wish was granted, and during the funeral procession to Assisi, they made a detour via San Damiano, where Francis' body was placed near the choir grille window. Despite her illness, Clare allowed herself to be carried to the small opening, where she could kiss the visible sacred and stigmatic wound in Francis' hand and bid him farewell.

From this moment onward, Clare, known as "The Little Plant" of St. Francis, experienced profound spiritual growth. Her understanding deepened as she spent long hours meditating on the "original poverty" exemplified by the infant Jesus, the Babe of Bethlehem, wrapped in the humble poverty of a simple manger. Clare would go on to beautifully reveal much of her inner life through her famous and preserved writings.

The Spirituality of Clare and Her Letters

The serene and peaceful atmosphere of San Damiano must have provided the perfect backdrop for the act of putting pen to paper. As we've recounted earlier, during his prolonged agony, Francis took some time to compose his renowned Canticles, drawing inspiration from the landscape, nature, and wildlife. In Cologne, Germany, there resided a truly holy young woman named Ermentrude, who lived a virtuous life. After losing her parents, she prayed and sought God's guidance for her calling. Through divine will and advice from her Dominican priest, she embarked on a journey to find a community of virgins. Her travels led her to the delightful city of Bruges in Belgium, where she felt her journey had reached its destination. In time, Ermentrude's community grew as other young girls joined her, forming the "Disciples of Christ."

Without a specific religious Rule to follow, Ermentrude prayed for guidance, and it was then that she reached out to Clare, seeking her advice. Despite the option of sending an Abbess to oversee the development of this new community, Clare, ever humble, recognized that the best service would come from within. Her response to Ermentrude's request was a beautiful letter filled with simple yet profound words. All of

Clare's letters and writings came from the depths of her heart, directed either to individuals or her own community of sisters. However, as we delve into them, it becomes evident that they could apply to anyone, to all, even to us in our modern world.

Clare's faithfulness was a significant virtue, and by being "faithful to Him," Jesus would lead to the "Crown of Everlasting Life" through the daily labors in this world. Her message was straightforward: dedicate your life, work, and leisure to God with humility, and He will reward you with eternal blessings. Clare herself spent long hours meditating on the mysteries of the cross, the Passion of the Lord, and the anguish of Mary standing beneath the Cross, urging us to do the same. She reminded us to be "vigilant" and cautious against deceit in its many forms, encouraging us to close our eyes and ears to flattery and worldly temptations. It is through prayer and supporting each other's burdens that we fulfill Christ's laws.

Ermentrude's heart was filled with joy and encouragement upon receiving Clare's letter, and she introduced the Rule of San Damiano to her growing community. After Clare's passing, Ermentrude sought approval from the Pope to expand the Order to Belgium and the northern provinces of France, establishing more monasteries. Today, we can hardly fathom the significance of letter writing. We rarely find time to sit and gather our thoughts, and our advice to loved ones often stems from external motivations rather than heartfelt intentions.

In the 1230s, Clare wrote her first three letters to Agnes of Prague, who, like Clare, would later be elevated to sainthood. Given the challenges of communication in those times, many letters would have passed back and forth between these two saints, carried by priests or friars on arduous journeys. Agnes, born in Prague in 1200, was a princess and the daughter of the

King of Bohemia. Despite the advances and marriage proposals from kings and princes, Agnes longed for a life of prayer and solitude. With Pope Gregory IX's intervention, she found her freedom and established the "Daughters of St. Clare" in Prague, along with a Franciscan Church and hospital.

Clare's letters to Agnes revealed her profound love for Christ and her deep appreciation for poverty, which she often mentioned, saying, "I possess that which I most desire under heaven." Poverty was the treasure that brought Clare the greatest joy. She understood that Jesus himself was "despised, needy, and poor in this world," and those who embrace poverty can become "rich in Him" by possessing the Kingdom of Heaven. Clare sought to accumulate treasures in heaven, knowing that eternal glory awaited those who embraced poverty. With her eyes fixed on the poor and crucified Christ, Clare offered everything to God the Father, united to Jesus, encouraging us to "Love Him who gave Himself totally out of love for you." In her life and letters, Clare and her sisters showed sensitivity to the needs of others, sharing their burdens, difficulties, and sufferings.

Clare closely followed and was united to Mary, the Mother of Christ, encouraging us to love and cling to her, just as Mary offered her own virgin body to God and carried Jesus in her sacred womb through the power of the Holy Spirit. In Clare's fourth and final known letter to Agnes, written in 1252 during the last months of Clare's life, she shares her great joy in participating in the Eucharist, calling it a "sacred banquet." Joy serves as an antidote and shield against darkness and pain. Clare speaks poetically of Jesus' generosity and the promise of resurrection, leading to everlasting glory. She uses the metaphor of Christ being a mirror without tarnish, reflecting ourselves back to us, encouraging us to gaze into this mirror every day."

The Rule of the Order of Poor Clare's

During their time at San Damiano, the Poor Clare's lived according to the Rule or "Form of Life" that Francis had taught them, with some additions made by two successive Popes. As new monasteries began to thrive in various places near and far, Clare recognized the need to compose a Rule specifically tailored to her Order, one that could be strictly adhered to. In doing so, Clare achieved a historical feat as the first woman to create a Religious Rule in the Church's history.

The process of writing the Rule spanned five years, starting in 1247, and its twelve chapters laid down the definitive Franciscan way of life. Right from the first chapter, Clare emphasized the primary values: living in obedience, without personal possessions, and in chastity, all while observing the Holy Gospel of Jesus Christ. The ideals cherished by Francis, the ways of Jesus, were to be faithfully put into practice. The sisters were to console the afflicted, care for the sick, and embrace absolute holy poverty by renouncing any form of ownership.

The Rule itself is presented in a straightforward and concise manner, encompassing all aspects of a sister's vocation and the commitments it entails. It culminates with a reaffirmation to perpetually observe the poverty and humility of Jesus Christ, His Holy Mother, and the Holy Gospel.

In her Rule, Clare sets an example of holiness, nourished by prayer, leading to the contemplation of God's very essence. Opening one's heart to the Holy Spirit results in a transformation towards love and peace in thought and action. This vocation becomes a radiant testament to those in the world, a shining witness of living in accordance with the Gospel principles.

Clare's Personal Testament, Prayers, and Blessing

After Francis' passing, Clare continued to live in this world for another twenty-seven years, taking on the role of custodian and defender of his example, principles, and teachings. Toward the end of her life, Clare dictated what could be considered her "Last Will and Testament." This sacred document, recorded "In the name of the Lord," expressed her heartfelt gratitude to God. In her Testament, Clare emphasized the Father's merciful love and kindness, firmly believing in the power of reciprocal love within a community. She urged her followers to "Love one another with the charity of Christ, and let the love in your hearts be outwardly demonstrated through your actions."

One of Clare's known compositions is a long prayer that she recited daily with fervor and devotion, honoring the five wounds of the Lord. During these moments, Clare would fix her gaze upon the poor and crucified Christ, pouring out her heart in supplication.

The well-known Blessing of St. Clare, bestowed upon her sisters, has become widely familiar today. However, it is actually a condensed version of the original blessing, adapted in various ways for more universal use. In additional lines from her prayer of blessing, Clare assured her sisters, "I bless you during my life and after my death. I leave you all the blessings that I can give you, and I implore them from God Who lives and reigns the world without end. Amen." This promise of intercession from heaven after her passing provides reassurance to those she left behind.

San Damiano: Later Years - Penance, Fasting, and Prayer

Throughout her life, Clare devoted herself to penance, prayer, and fasting, offering it all to her Savior. Her form of penance involved rigorous self-mortification, which might be considered extreme by today's standards. The habit she wore was coarse and rough, serving more as a covering than a source of warmth. Clare never wore shoes, and her feet always remained bare. Under her habit, she wore a hair shirt, at times even choosing one made of sharp and prickly pig bristles. Her bed was simply ground, with a layer of vines as a mattress and a wooden block as a pillow. As her body weakened with time, she reluctantly allowed herself a little straw for her head, only complying with this practice later in obedience to Francis's guidance.

Clare's fasting and abstinence were so rigorous that it seemed only supernatural forces kept her alive. During the long Lenten periods (including most of November and December, known as the Lent of St. Martin), Clare would consume nothing at all on Mondays, Wednesdays, and Fridays. On other days, she would sustain herself with only bread and water, allowing a little wine on Sundays. The years of such strict fasting took a toll on her body, leading to various infirmities. Eventually, at the insistence of both Francis and the Bishop, Clare was required to eat at least one and a half ounces of bread daily. However, what she lacked in physical nourishment, she compensated with contemplative acts of prayer and divine praises to God. Her unwavering gaze directed toward heaven allowed her to receive showers of Divine grace.

After Compline (night prayer), while all the other sisters

retired to their cells, Clare would continue her watchful prayer through the night, often prostrating herself on the floor, weeping tears of devotion at the feet of Christ. On one such night, the devil attacked her, appearing in the form of a small child. He warned Clare that her tears would cause blindness, to which she fearlessly replied, "Those who shall see God will not be blind." The dark angel then returned after midnight, warning her that her weeping would cause her brain to soften and deform her nose. Clare confidently replied, "Those who serve the Lord need not fear anything," causing the devil to vanish instantly.

Upon her return from these prolonged vigils, the community noticed such radiant joy and happiness in Clare's countenance that, during the canonization process, they testified, "Her face was more beautiful than the sun when she came back from prayers." Clare's devotion to her sisters extended beyond prayer as well; she was the last to sleep each night and the first to rise each morning, lighting the lanterns and preparing Morning Prayer, exemplifying Spirit-filled charity and love.

Amid all her ascetic practices, Clare held another great love: the Most Holy Eucharist.

The Power of the Eucharist

Clare's life revolved around the pure Bread of Heaven, the real Body of Jesus Christ in the Eucharist. In accordance with the customs of her time, she could only receive Holy Communion seven times a year. It's important to note that Francis, by his own choice, never sought ordination to the priesthood, so he couldn't celebrate Mass at San Damiano or elsewhere.

Pope Saint John Paul II once referred to Clare as a "eucharist," as she continually offered thanksgiving to God through her prayer, praise, love, and sacrifices from behind the cloistered walls. Though icons depict Clare holding a monstrance on the monastery walls, defending her community, that event didn't occur as visually depicted. Nevertheless, reality is equally powerful.

In September 1240, Emperor Frederick II of Germany, excommunicated multiple times, launched a campaign against parts of Italy allied with the Pope. Christian sanctuaries like Umbria and Assisi were prime targets. The army arrived at Assisi and surrounded San Damiano's walls. As the soldiers breached the outer walls and entered the cloisters, the sisters sought refuge with their ailing holy mother, Clare. Despite her illness, Clare reassured them, saying, "Do not be afraid, for if the Lord is with us, the enemy cannot harm us." The sisters brought Clare to the Blessed Sacrament. As the soldiers tried to break down the refectory door, Clare held the silver pyx containing the Blessed Sacrament as a shield. Prostrating herself, she tearfully implored God to defend and deliver her family from the invaders. A child's voice emanated from the pyx, declaring, "I will protect you always." Clare also asked for Assisi's defense, and the response came, "The city will be troubled, but shall be defended by My protection and your intercession." Trusting in the Lord, the Saracen forces mysteriously retreated and disappeared, overwhelmed by Clare's prayers. In the following year, the Imperial troops under Captain Vitalis of Aversa attacked Assisi, but Clare and her sisters' prayers once again led to victory.

The power of her prayers was renowned, not only for defeating armies but also for conquering the forces of darkness.

A woman from Pisa visited Clare to express her gratitude because, through Clare's intercession, five demons had been cast out. These evil spirits confessed that the saint's prayers had tormented them fearfully. Bishop Hugolino, later Cardinal and Pope Gregory IX, had great faith in Clare's prayers and often sought her intercession, always benefiting from her assistance in times of need. Clare's deep devotion to the Blessed Sacrament led her to turn to the real presence of Jesus in times of crisis, and His immediate help was always given.

The Sacred Sign of the Cross

The cherished symbol of the Franciscan Order, Saint Damian's Cross, hangs above the altar at San Damiano. Unlike the traditional crucifix with the nailed corpus of Christ, this painted icon in the Syrian style stands six feet tall. It was this very Cross that spoke to Francis and drew Clare into an intimate and profound understanding of God. Christ's gaze encompasses the entire world, His eyes wide open, portraying His crucifixion without sadness or pain. Instead, the unknown 12th-century artist transfigured the colors, radiating a luminosity that expresses the complete Paschal Mystery: Christ's death, resurrection, and ascension.

Clare's deep adoration for the crucified Jesus brought divine rewards. Her profound love for the mystery of the cross gifted her with the ability to perform miracles simply by making the Sign of the Cross. Whenever she made this sacred sign over a sick person, instant healing occurred. For instance, Brother Stephen, afflicted by insanity, was cured when Clare made the sign over him. Similarly, a three-year-old named Mattiolo, close to suffocation due to a lodged pebble, found relief and healing through Clare's touch. Another boy, suffering from a large sore covering his eye, regained his sight after receiving Clare's saintly blessing.

Within her own community, Clare's sign of the cross also brought miraculous healing. Sister Benvenuta's malignant ulcers were cured, as were Sister Amata's dropsy and violent coughing fits. Sister Christina, who had lost her ability to speak, regained her voice after Clare's intervention.

On a particular occasion, when the monastery's infirmary was filled with sick sisters, Clare visited and made the sign of the cross in the air five times. To everyone's astonishment, all five sisters rose from their sick beds, having received Clare's healing remedy. Drawing from the heart of Jesus, pierced with a lance, Clare accessed the healing power, which she transmitted to those who suffered. Her profound empathy and unwavering faith allowed Christ to heal through her as she made the sign of the cross.

Even Pope Gregory IX witnessed these signs during his visit to Assisi. After consulting with Clare on heavenly matters, he asked her to bless the baked bread rolls meant for him. In humble obedience, Clare made the sign of the cross over the loaves, and miraculously, each one bore an imprinted cross.

Clare's Love for Jesus and Her Sisters

Clare's heart was immersed in daily grief over the Lord's Passion, and she imparted this deep devotion to her novice daughters. As she contemplated the Crucified Christ, her heart overflowed with compassion, extending to everyone around her and fueling her prayers for the salvation of souls. Leading by example, Clare often shed tears in the seclusion of her cell, displaying her intense devotion to the five wounds of the crucified Christ. Even when the devil tried to deter her with brutal force, Clare's determination in prayer only grew stronger.

During one Easter season, Clare secluded herself in her cell to meditate on the Last Supper, remaining transfixed in remembrance of the Lord's suffering from Maundy Thursday until the end of Good Friday. Her profound desire was to know Christ and partake in His sufferings to reproduce the pattern of His death, as expressed in Philippians 3:10.

Clare instructed the sisters with both discipline and love, teaching them to meditate solely on God, to let go of their past lives and earthly attachments to please Christ, to overcome the temptations of the evil one, and to engage in manual labor. She arranged for visiting preachers so that all could regularly hear the Word of God. During one of these sessions, a serene heavenly child appeared at Clare's side while a Brother was preaching, enveloped in a brilliant light and exuding a sweet fragrance. Sister Agnes of Spello witnessed this heavenly encounter and heard the child Jesus' sweet voice, affirming His presence among them.

Clare's understanding of God's compassion and humility for humanity led her to practice self-emptying, making her heart available to share the suffering of others. True humility, characterized by fearlessness and reliance on God, was the foundation of her spiritual life. Clare fearlessly confronted challenges, including resisting offers of land and revenues from Popes and Cardinals, remaining steadfast in following Christ's teachings.

As an Abbess, Clare's union with God was evident in the way she attended to the welfare and needs of all the sisters.

She showed understanding and compassion, allowing for a less rigorous path for those who couldn't cope with strict observances. When sisters faced temptations, Clare consoled them with tears and humbly placed herself at their feet in sorrow. The community deeply admired and respected their Superior, striving to follow her path of perfection.

Clare's Sickness and Final Days

Throughout the last twenty-seven years of her life, almost half her total years, Clare endured a mysterious illness that brought forth various infirmities, leaving her weak and bedridden. Despite her physical suffering, Clare never once complained about her sickness or the poverty she willingly embraced. Her joy in serving the Lord was boundless, and she proclaimed, "Can a heart which possesses the infinite God be truly called poor?" Even on Christmas Eve, when Clare was confined to her bed while the other sisters went to the chapel, Jesus rewarded her devotion by coming to her in her suffering. At midnight, as the Christ Child's nativity unfolded, Clare heard the heavenly music and hymns from St. Francis Church, carried miraculously to her at San Damiano. Not only did she hear the praises, but she was granted the supernatural grace to witness the events at St. Francis Church, seeing the crib and the Holy Infant Child Jesus lying in the manger. Celestially transported, she participated in the Mass and received Holy Communion before returning to her bed.

As 1251 approached, Clare's medical condition worsened, and she found herself confined to her small bed. The rigors of her austere lifestyle had taken their toll, leaving her weakened and fatigued. Nonetheless, even from her sickbed, Clare continued to work for God. While heavy manual tasks were beyond her ability, a sister arranged for her comfort, providing a pillow to allow Clare to sit upright. Using her healing fingers, Clare used fine linens to intricately spin dozens of corporals, which were wrapped in silk cases and given to the Franciscan Brothers. These altar cloths, now sanctified by her touch, were distributed to poorer churches in the surrounding Umbrian mountains, hills, and valleys.

During her time of bed rest, Sister Amata took care of Clare and noticed a remarkable change in her demeanor. From appearing pale and worn, Clare's features suddenly beamed with happiness and smiles. When asked about this transformation, Clare revealed that she rejoiced because she held her dearest Lord in her arms, who was the joy of her soul. Christian joy, a virtue stemming from victory over suffering, radiated from Clare's soul, a gift of grace from heaven, mediated by the Lord Himself. In that moment, Jesus revealed His presence to Sister Amata, filling her with enraptured joy as well.

The Pope's Arrival and Clare's Rule Confirmation

In Saint Clare's final days, her unwavering devotion and continuous prayers filled the air. As her health declined, a remarkable vision foretold the arrival of the Pope and his disciples. It was during this time that Pope Innocent IV, who had been residing in Lyon due to conflicts in Italy, decided to return to Perugia. Hearing of Clare's serious condition, Cardinal Raynaldus, a close friend and advisor, rushed to her side. He administered Holy Communion and offered his blessings to

Clare and her sisters.

Throughout her illness, Clare's deepest desire was for the Pope to confirm and approve her Rule for the Order of Poor Ladies. Cardinal Raynaldus, faithful to his promise, sought to fulfill her wish. Yet, a year passed, and Clare patiently awaited the longed-for confirmation. Then, a significant event brought hope—the Papal party arrived in Assisi to consecrate the Basilica of St. Francis.

Pope Innocent IV, accompanied by his entourage of Cardinals, hastened to visit the beloved servant of Christ. With utmost reverence, Clare greeted the Pontiff, humbly kissing his feet. Filled with gratitude, she sought pardon and full remission of her sins from the Holy Father. He, in turn, granted her absolution and apostolic benediction, culminating in Clare receiving Holy Communion.

After the dignitaries departed, Clare lifted her tear-filled eyes towards heaven and praised the Lord. She rejoiced in the granting of her fervent wish—communion with Christ and the presence of His Vicar on earth. However, her mortal journey was not yet over, and Clare continued to endure her final agony for nearly three more weeks.

During this time, her devoted community surrounded her, tears flowing ceaselessly. Her sister, Abbess Agnes, returned to be by her side, and Clare, with her characteristic gift of prophecy, assured her of a comforting consolation before her own passing, a prophecy that later came true.

Though she could not eat for seventeen days, Clare remained steadfast, comforting her followers and expressing her enduring love for Christ. She requested to hear the Lord's Passion and reminded her holy daughters to cherish praise and thanksgiving. The wait for her Rule's written approval finally came to an end, as the Papal Bull arrived and was placed in her hands. Overwhelmed with devotion, Clare kissed the document, and a sense of peace enveloped her. With the confirmation of her Rule, Clare could now embrace the fulfillment of her life's mission.

As her strength waned, two of Saint Francis' closest companions, Brother Leo and Brother Angelo, paid their respects. Brother Leo, Francis' confessor and advisor, tenderly kissed Clare's bed, while Brother Angelo consoled the other nuns.

On Saturday, August 10th, 1253, Saint Clare clung to life, her soul yearning to meet her Creator. Her fervent wish had come true, and she could now rest assured that her Rule would endure for all time. The Papal Bull, carefully signed in Assisi, was a testament to the lasting impact of her legacy.

Throughout her suffering, Clare's steadfast faith never wavered. Despite her physical afflictions, she remained unwavering in her devotion to the Lord. With her Rule confirmed and her heart at peace, Saint Clare embraced the final moments of her earthly journey. She left behind a profound example of humility, love, and dedication to God, inspiring countless souls to follow in her footsteps.

As Saint Clare prepared to depart this world, her sisters gathered around her, finding strength in her words and example. She imparted her wisdom one last time, reminding them of the divine benefits that flow from praise and thanksgiving. Clare's words served as a guiding light for her holy daughters of poverty, urging them to continue their spiritual journey with fervor and grace.

With each passing moment, Clare's life on earth drew to a

close. Surrounded by her beloved community, she finally let go, surrendering her soul to God's embrace. As the heavens welcomed a new saint, the world mourned the loss of a cherished and revered spiritual leader.

The legacy of Saint Clare endured beyond her physical presence. Her Order continued to flourish, spreading across lands and generations, guided by the Rule she had penned with unwavering devotion. Her remarkable life and the enduring impact of her legacy echoed through the annals of history, leaving an indelible mark on the hearts of the faithful.

In the heavenly realms, Saint Clare found eternal rest and joy in the company of the Virgin Mary and the saints. Her arduous earthly journey had led her to the embrace of her Beloved, and now, in the Palaces of the Heavenly Mansions, she experienced the ultimate fulfillment of her heart's desire. Saint Clare's soul was at peace, forever basking in the divine light and love of her Lord and Savior, Jesus Christ.

A Holy Departure and Burial

During the late hours of Friday, August 9th, as the sisters kept a vigil by Clare's bedside, they testified to hearing her speak calmly and lucidly to her own soul, as if reciting her own Magnificat. She said, "Go forth in peace, for you will have good company on your journey. Go forth, for He Who created you has sanctified you and protected you with a mother's tender love." Clare then prayed, "Thank you, Lord, for having created me."

Throughout the night, Clare fervently prayed her favorite devotion to the Five Wounds of Christ. In her final words to Sister Agnes, she said, "Precious in the sight of the Lord is the death of his holy ones." During these sacred moments of her passage, a miraculous vision unfolded. Sister Benvenuta saw a procession of Virgins dressed in white robes and golden crowns walking towards the monastery door. Among them was one even greater and more beautiful—the Blessed Virgin Mary. Her crown emitted a brilliant luminance that turned night into day. Mary approached Clare's bed, embraced her lovingly, and covered her with an exquisite cloth. The two became indistinguishable, and the room became radiant with adornment. Clare's contemplative journey was reaching its end, culminating in her vision of the "King of Glory."

On the evening of August 11th, 1253, with the summer light fading, Clare passed peacefully from this life to the clarity of eternal light. It was the feast day of Saint Ruffino, Assisi's patron, and Sister Filippa, Clare's lifelong friend, described how Clare departed without stain or darkness of sin.

The news of Clare's passing spread quickly, and the people of Assisi rushed to San Damiano. The mayor and city knights kept vigil around their beloved lady. The next day, the Pope, Cardinals, and Priests gathered to celebrate the Funeral Mass. Pope Innocent IV was eager to canonize her immediately, but Cardinal Raynaldus persuaded him to reflect further on her holiness. After the funeral rites, Clare's holy remains were carried on a bier and buried in the Church of St. George by Assisi's eastern gate.

Causes Miracles and Canonisation

After Clare's passing, Pope Innocent IV wasted no time in initiating the process of her canonization. He appointed the Bishop of Spoleto as the postulator, along with the assistance of the Franciscan Friars, Leo and Angelo, and others. The team was sent to San Damiano to interview the sisters who personally knew Clare, and they also gathered testimonies from citizens of Assisi and surrounding areas who had known Clare or experienced her intercession and miracles. The testimonies attested to Clare's sanctity, her love for the poor, her honesty, kindness, humility, and compassion for others' physical and spiritual needs.

During this examination of her sanctity, numerous miracles were recorded and attributed to Clare after her death. People suffering from various afflictions found healing and restoration at her tomb. A boy plagued by possession, others with paralysis, contracted legs, epilepsy, wasting diseases, and cancer, were all miraculously cured. Children who were chronically disabled, unable to walk, found restoration through Clare's intercession. Some were saved from dire situations, like children rescued from wolves' jaws. Tumors and cancers vanished, and the blind regained their sight after Clare appeared to them in dreams.

In the months following Clare's death, her reputation as a holy and miraculous woman spread worldwide. The new Pope Alexander IV, formerly Cardinal Raynaldus, led the commission to examine Clare's life. The commission unanimously agreed that Clare's life was a shining example of virtue and that her miracles were real and proven. They concluded that Clare deserved to be glorified on earth, as God had already glorified her in heaven.

Only two years after Clare's death, a grand celebration took place at the Cathedral in Agnani, forty miles southeast of Rome, where thousands gathered. Pope Alexander IV praised Clare as a clear and shining light, a princess of the poor, and declared her a saint before the multitudes, elevating her to the realm of Sainthood.

Assisi today- St. Clare's Body and Basilica

After St. Clare's death, her body was interred in the Church of Saint George in the eastern part of Assisi to safeguard it from potential thieves who would take relics for veneration elsewhere. However, as pilgrims from far and wide began to visit her resting place, it became apparent that a more suitable home was needed for the great saint. Hence, the inhabitants of Assisi decided to construct a grand church and monastery, which was completed seven years later in 1260. On the Feast of St. Francis, Pope Alexander IV presided over the translation of St. Clare's body to its new resting place in the newly built Church of St. Clare.

When the tomb was opened, seven years after her death, St. Clare's body was found to be completely incorrupt, as if she had just fallen asleep. Her body was placed in a stone coffin beneath the High Altar and the Cathedral was dedicated to St. Clare on the same day. In 1265, it was consecrated and became the Basilica of St. Clare. Centuries later, in 1850, with permission from the Holy See and the desire to bring her closer to the public, her tomb was opened again, and a new place of veneration was created within the Basilica. In this process, they found the original Rule for her Order, which she wrote in her own hand, hidden in the folds of her mantle.

The Basilica of St. Clare is made of unique pink stone from Mount Subasio, and its façade features a large circular rose window that bathes the interior in a soft gauze of light. The basilica offers a stunning panoramic view across the Umbrian valley. Inside, visitors can find the Chapel of the San Damiano Cross, where the iconic crucifix that spoke to St. Francis and under which St. Clare spent most of her life is displayed. Opposite this chapel lies the burial place of St. Clare's mother and sister, Blessed Ortolana and St. Agnes. The crypt, accessible through stairs from the center of the basilica, houses a lifelike mold encasing St. Clare's body, protecting it while preserving her appearance for veneration. Visitors can also see relics such as St. Clare's golden locks of hair, hair shirt, mantle, and habit.

Today, the Basilica of St. Clare stands as a revered place of pilgrimage, honoring the memory of this remarkable saint who dedicated her life to serving God and helping others.

Walking in St. Clare's footsteps to San Damiano

Assisi, a well-preserved city, offers a unique opportunity for pilgrims to step back in time and follow in the footsteps of the saints who once walked its paths and squares. The city is mostly traffic-free, allowing visitors to explore on foot. While many tourists head straight to the three-tiered Basilica of St. Francis at the western end of Assisi, those seeking a deeper spiritual experience may find solace in the quieter surroundings of the Basilica of St. Clare.

To truly absorb the spirituality of Assisi, it is recommended to spend at least two or three full days in the city. The journey in St. Clare's footsteps starts at her house, where she would leave to attend Mass at San Ruffino. The original cathedral of Assisi, San Ruffino was constructed in 1140, and its baptismal font holds special significance as it was where both Saints Clare and Francis were baptized.

To reach the foot of the hill where St. Clare fled to the Porziuncula, visitors can take a short bus trip or walk up the newly built pilgrims' steps. The Porziuncula, situated in the enormous Basilica of Saint Mary of the Angels, is a crucial location in the life of St. Francis. The basilica, dominating the valley, houses the small church where St. Francis resided.

For a relatively short and scenic walk, pilgrims can reach the Monastery and Church of San Damiano through the eastern gate of Assisi. Clare's deep love for all of creation is evident in the teachings she imparted to the sisters serving outside the walls—to praise God when they see the beauty of nature and all living beings.

The Monastery of San Damiano, currently cared for by the Franciscan Friars, is a haven of peace and tranquility amid olive groves. The cloisters, garden, and courtyard offer a serene environment to reflect and find inner calm. The chapel, where Mass is still celebrated each morning, the refectory, and St. Clare's cell with their original furnishings preserve a tangible link to the past, making this a center of spirituality. It is a place to meditate on Psalm 16:11, "You will reveal the path of life to me, give me unbounded joy in your presence."

Visiting these sacred places in Assisi allows pilgrims to immerse themselves in the spiritual legacy of St. Clare and experience the profound serenity and wisdom she left behind.

St. Clare's Patronage and Legacy

Saint Clare's Feast Day is celebrated on August 11th, although originally it was on August 12th, coinciding with the feast day of Assisi's patron saint, Ruffino. Today, St. Clare is not only revered as a patron by the faithful citizens of Assisi but also holds patronage over various areas. She is known as the patron saint of eye disease and eyes due to her miraculous intercession, as mentioned earlier. Additionally, she is the patron of embroiderers (needlework) for her ability to spin fine corporals even in her infirm state. In a more modern recognition, Pope Pius XII declared her the patron saint of television because of a Christmas miracle where she witnessed the Midnight Mass projected on her wall and heard the liturgy despite being bedridden.

During her lifetime, St. Clare founded 153 monasteries for her Order, and today there are over 900 monasteries in 76 countries with more than 20,000 Poor Clare Sisters.

In the twenty-first century, St. Clare's teachings remain relevant and serve as a guiding light for us. She would never seek the title of "Great Saint," as her greatness lay in her profound humility. Drawing inspiration from scripture, she encouraged others to carry out their duties without complaint or argument, shining like bright stars in the world (Philippians 2:14–16). Her way of life and spiritual legacy are invaluable treasures that she invites us to embrace, always striving to imitate the path of holy simplicity and humility.

Prayer composed by St. Clare in honor of the five wounds of the Lord

1. In praise and adoration, I lift my heart to You, O Lord Jesus Christ, for the sacred wound in Your right hand. By this hallowed wound, I implore Your forgiveness for all my sins—those committed through thoughts, words, and deeds. May Your boundless love and sacrifice inspire me to remember Your Holy Passion fervently and honor Your sacred wounds. Grant me the strength to demonstrate my gratitude through self-discipline, acknowledging Your sufferings and death. Amen.

2. My dearest Jesus, I offer my praises and gratitude for the sacred wound in Your left hand. I humbly ask for Your mercy to transform all that displeases You within me. Grant me victory over all adversaries through Your grace, and safeguard me from present and future dangers by the power of Your loving death. May Your holy sacrifice lead me to share in the glory of Your Blessed Kingdom. Amen.

3. O sweetest Jesus, I lift my voice in praise and thanksgiving for the sacred wound in Your right foot. By this divine wound, I seek the strength to perform good works as a penance for my sins. Guide me day and night according to Your holy will, shielding me from afflictions of body and soul. On the day of judgement, grant me Your mercy, that I may attain eternal happiness. Amen.

4. My gracious Jesus, I adore and thank You for the sacred wound in Your left foot. Through this loving wound, I beseech Your forgiveness and complete pardon for all my sins. By

Your grace, may I always avoid Your justice and embrace Your boundless mercy. At the hour of my death, grant me the grace of perfect contrition and the reception of the Sacraments for my eternal salvation. Amen.

5. O good and merciful Jesus, I lift my heart in praise for the sacred wound in Your side. Your immense mercy was shown not only to Longinus, the centurion who pierced Your side, but also to all of us, cleansing us from original sin in Baptism. By the merits of Your Precious Blood, delivered over the world this day, deliver me from all evils—past, present, and future. Grant me a fervent faith, unwavering hope, and perfect love, so that I may love You with my whole being and glorify Your name for all eternity. Amen.

Let us Pray

O powerful and everlasting God, who, through the five wounds of Your Son, our Lord, and Savior Jesus Christ, redeemed humanity, we humbly implore You, by the merits of His Precious Blood, to bestow upon us the grace of protection from sudden and unprepared death. As we honor and revere these loving wounds daily, may we find solace and security in Your boundless love.

We offer this prayer through our Lord Jesus Christ, Your Son, who, together with You and the Holy Spirit, reigns as one God for all eternity. Amen.

Novena in Reverence of Saint Clare In Anticipation of Her Feast Day(August 2nd until August 10th)

Day 1

Let us commence this sacred journey, invoking the divine presence of the Father, the Son, and the Holy Spirit. Amen.

O most Holy Trinity, Father, Son, and Holy Spirit, we offer our heartfelt praise for the wondrous grace manifested in your devoted servant, St. Clare. Through her potent intercession, grant us the blessings we seek during this Novena, above all, the grace to emulate her life of profound love for you. Amen.

O Seraphic St. Clare, the first follower of the Poor Man of Assisi, who willingly renounced all wealth and honors for a life of sacrifice and utmost humility, we implore you to obtain from God the grace of surrendering to the Divine Will and confidently trusting in the providence of our Heavenly Father.

(Share your personal supplications here.)

Pray for us, St. Clare,
   that we may be deemed worthy of Christ's promises.

Lord, we beseech You, grant us, your devoted servants who honor the Feast of St. Clare, your Virgin, to partake in the celestial joys of heaven and become co-heirs with your only begotten Son, who, as God, reigns eternally. Amen.

O glorious St. Clare! God has bestowed upon you the power to work miracles ceaselessly, and the privilege of hearing the prayers of those who invoke your aid in times of hardship, anxiety, and distress. We earnestly beseech you to intercede for us before Jesus, through the blessed intercession of His Mother Mary, so that our fervent and hopeful pleas may be granted, always for the greater glory of God and the salvation of our souls. Amen.

In the name of the Father, the Son, and the Holy Spirit. Amen.

Day 2

Let us commence our prayers, invoking the divine presence of the Father, the Son, and the Holy Spirit. Amen.

O most Holy Trinity, Father, Son, and Holy Spirit, we offer our heartfelt adoration for the marvelous grace manifested in your devoted servant, St. Clare. Through her powerful intercession, may the blessings we seek in this Novena be granted, above all, the grace to embrace and depart from this world with the same fervent love she held for you. Amen.

O Seraphic St. Clare, whose heart remains ever compassionate towards the poor and afflicted, assuming the role of a nurturing mother to them, forsaking your own wealth to work innumerable miracles for their sake, we implore you to obtain from God the grace of Christian charity towards others, tending to their spiritual and material needs.

(Share your personal supplications here.)

Pray for us, St. Clare,
    that we may be deemed worthy of Christ's promises.

Lord, we beseech You, grant us, your devoted servants who honor the Feast of St. Clare, your Virgin, to partake in the celestial joys of heaven and become co-heirs with your only begotten Son, who, as God, reigns eternally. Amen.

O glorious St. Clare! God has bestowed upon you the power to work miracles ceaselessly, and the favor of answering the prayers of those who invoke your aid in times of misfortune, anxiety, and distress. We earnestly implore you to intercede for us before Jesus, through the blessed intercession of His Mother Mary, so that our fervent and hopeful pleas may be granted, always for the greater glory of God and the betterment of our souls. Amen.

In the name of the Father, the Son, and the Holy Spirit. Amen.

Day 3

Let us embark on this day's devotions, invoking the divine presence of the Father, the Son, and the Holy Spirit. Amen.

O most Holy Trinity, Father, Son, and Holy Spirit, we offer reverent praise for the marvelous grace bestowed upon your servant, St. Clare. Through her powerful intercession, may the favors we seek in this Novena be granted, above all, the grace to live and depart from this world immersed in your divine love. Amen.

O Seraphic St. Clare, illustrious beacon of your homeland, instrumental in delivering Italy from ruthless invaders, we beseech you to obtain from God the grace of overcoming all threats to our faith and morals. By doing so, may our families be blessed with true Christian harmony, a profound fear of God, and unwavering devotion to the Blessed Sacrament.

(Share your personal supplications here.)

Pray for us, St. Clare,
   that we may be deemed worthy of Christ's promises.

Lord, we entreat You, grant us, your devoted servants who honor the Feast of St. Clare, your Virgin, to partake in the celestial joys of heaven and become co-heirs with your only begotten Son, who, as God, reigns eternally. Amen.

O glorious St. Clare! God has bestowed upon you the continuous power to work miracles and the gracious favor of answering the prayers of those who seek your assistance in times of misfortune, anxiety, and distress. We earnestly plead with you to intercede for us before Jesus, through the blessed intercession of His Mother Mary, so that our fervent and hopeful entreaties may be fulfilled, always for the greater glory of God and the betterment of our souls. Amen.

In the name of the Father, the Son, and the Holy Spirit. Amen.

Day 4

Let us commence this day's devotion, invoking the divine presence of the Father, the Son, and the Holy Spirit. Amen.

O most Holy Trinity, Father, Son, and Holy Spirit, we offer our heartfelt praise for the wondrous grace manifested in your servant, St. Clare. Through her powerful intercession, may the favors we seek in this Novena be granted, above all, the grace to lead lives immersed in your holiest love and to find solace in it even in death. Amen.

Blessed St. Clare, whose very name signifies illumination, enlighten the darkness shrouding our minds and hearts, guiding us towards discerning God's will, and inspiring us to fulfill it with joy and willingness. As a prophetic voice heralded your coming into this world as a radiant light, be a guiding beacon for us amidst the sorrows and anxieties of earthly existence, leading us towards the eternal light of our heavenly abode. Amen.

(Share your personal supplications here.)

Pray for us, St. Clare,

that we may be deemed worthy of Christ's promises.

Lord, we beseech You, grant us, your devoted servants who honor the Feast of St. Clare, your Virgin, to partake in the celestial joys of heaven and become co-heirs with your only begotten Son, who, as God, reigns eternally. Amen.

O glorious St. Clare! God has bestowed upon you the continuous power to work miracles and the gracious favor of answering the prayers of those who seek your assistance in times of misfortune, anxiety, and distress. We earnestly entreat you to intercede for us before Jesus, through the blessed intercession of His Mother Mary, so that our fervent and hopeful pleas may be granted, always for the greater glory of God and the betterment of our souls. Amen.

In the name of the Father, the Son, and the Holy Spirit. Amen.

Day 5

Let us commence this day's devotion, invoking the divine presence of the Father, the Son, and the Holy Spirit. Amen.

O most Holy Trinity, Father, Son, and Holy Spirit, we offer our heartfelt praise for the wondrous grace manifested in your servant, St. Clare. Through her powerful intercession, may the favors we seek in this Novena be granted, above all, the grace to lead lives immersed in your holiest love and to find solace in it even in death. Amen.

Seraphic St. Clare, whose heart overflowed with boundless love for the entire world, graciously accept our petitions into your pure hands and present them before God. Pray for us, so that one day, we may joyfully stand before the throne of God. Let the radiance of your immaculate purity dispel the shadows of sin and corruption that obscure our world. Intercede with your innocence on behalf of our youth. Safeguard the peace within our homes and foster unity within our families. Advocate with your chaste love for all those facing peril. Amen.

(Share your personal supplications here.)

Pray for us, St. Clare,
   that we may be deemed worthy of Christ's promises.

Lord, we entreat You, grant us, your devoted servants who honor the Feast of St. Clare, your Virgin, to partake in the celestial joys of heaven and become co-heirs with your only begotten Son, who, as God, reigns eternally. Amen.

O glorious St. Clare! God has bestowed upon you the continuous power to work miracles and the gracious favor of answering the prayers of those who seek your assistance in times of misfortune, anxiety, and distress. We earnestly beseech you to intercede for us before Jesus, through the blessed intercession of His Mother Mary, so that our fervent and hopeful pleas may be granted, always for the greater glory of God and the betterment of our souls. Amen.

In the name of the Father, the Son, and the Holy Spirit. Amen.

Day 6

Let us commence this day's devotion, invoking the divine presence of the Father, the Son, and the Holy Spirit. Amen.

O most Holy Trinity, Father, Son, and Holy Spirit, we offer our heartfelt praise for the wondrous grace manifested in your servant, St. Clare. Through her powerful intercession, may the favors we seek in this Novena be granted, above all, the grace to lead lives immersed in your holiest love and to find solace in it even in death. Amen.

Generous St. Clare, who relinquished wealth, earthly pleasures, and all material possessions to become the first spiritual daughter of St. Francis and serve God in the cloister, guides us to surrender our lives to God without reservation or measure. May He reside within us and radiate from us, touching the lives of all those we encounter. You, who loved souls so ardently that you made your life a continuous sacrifice for them, obtain for us the graces we seek and grant us the strength to praise God amidst both suffering and joy. Amen.

(Share your personal supplications here.)

Pray for us, St. Clare,
    that we may be deemed worthy of Christ's promises.

Lord, we entreat You, grant us, your devoted servants who honor the Feast of St. Clare, your Virgin, to partake in the celestial joys of heaven and become co-heirs with your only begotten Son, who, as God, reigns eternally. Amen.

O glorious St. Clare! God has bestowed upon you the continuous power to work miracles and the gracious favor of answering the prayers of those who seek your assistance in times of misfortune, anxiety, and distress. We earnestly implore you to intercede for us before Jesus, through the blessed intercession of His Mother Mary, so that our fervent and hopeful pleas may be granted, always for the greater glory of God and the betterment of our souls. Amen.

In the name of the Father, the Son, and the Holy Spirit. Amen.

Day 7

Let us embark on this day's devotion, invoking the divine presence of the Father, the Son, and the Holy Spirit. Amen.

O most Holy Trinity, Father, Son, and Holy Spirit, we offer our heartfelt praise for the wondrous grace manifested in your servant, St. Clare. Through her powerful intercession, may the favors we seek in this Novena be granted, above all, the grace to lead lives immersed in your holiest love and to find solace in it even in death. Amen.

Faithful St. Clare, devoted daughter of the Church, esteemed friend and confidante of popes, we beseech you to intercede for the well-being of the holy Church, and to look kindly upon our Holy Father, the Pope. Enlighten our souls, that we may remove any hindrances to the progress of the Church on Earth. Instill within us a profound love for God's Church, and may our lives contribute to the spreading of His kingdom on Earth through holy living. You, who worked miracles in the presence of the pope during your earthly journey, obtain for us the graces we now seek, as you stand in the presence of the Most High God in heaven. Amen.

(Share your personal supplications here.)

Pray for us, St. Clare,
  that we may be deemed worthy of Christ's promises.

Lord, we entreat You, grant us, your devoted servants who honor the Feast of St. Clare, your Virgin, to partake in the celestial joys of heaven and become co-heirs with your only begotten Son, who, as God, reigns eternally. Amen.

O glorious St. Clare! God has bestowed upon you the continuous power to work miracles and the gracious favor of answering the prayers of those who seek your assistance in times of misfortune, anxiety, and distress. We earnestly plead with you to intercede for us before Jesus, through the blessed intercession of His Mother Mary, so that our fervent and hopeful pleas may be fulfilled, always for the greater glory of God and the betterment of our souls. Amen.

In the name of the Father, the Son, and the Holy Spirit. Amen.

Day 8

Let us embark on this day's devotion, invoking the divine presence of the Father, the Son, and the Holy Spirit. Amen.

O most Holy Trinity, Father, Son, and Holy Spirit, we offer

our heartfelt praise for the wondrous grace manifested in your servant, St. Clare. Through her powerful intercession, may the favors we seek in this Novena be granted, above all, the grace to lead lives immersed in your holiest love and to find solace in it even in death. Amen.

Valiant St. Clare, who fearlessly stood firm against the barbarous Saracens, placing your unwavering trust in the Blessed Sacrament as your sole protection, ignite within us a deep love for Jesus Christ; guide us to live Eucharistic lives. You, who safeguarded your city of Assisi from devastation and ruin, extend your protection over our city and archdiocese, and intercede for our beloved country and the suffering world. A voice from the Sacred Heart rewarded your trust with a promise: "I will always take care of you." Glorious St. Clare, from your exalted place in heaven, now watch over us in our earthly needs and lead us towards heavenly light. Amen.

(Share your personal supplications here.)

Pray for us, St. Clare,
    that we may be deemed worthy of Christ's promises.

Lord, we entreat You, grant us, your devoted servants who honor the Feast of St. Clare, your Virgin, to partake in the celestial joys of heaven and become co-heirs with your only begotten Son, who, as God, reigns eternally. Amen.

O glorious St. Clare! God has bestowed upon you the continuous power to work miracles and the gracious favor of answering the prayers of those who seek your assistance in times of misfortune, anxiety, and distress. We earnestly implore you to intercede for us before Jesus, through the blessed intercession of His Mother Mary, so that our fervent and hopeful pleas may be fulfilled, always for the greater glory of God and the betterment of our souls. Amen.

In the name of the Father, the Son, and the Holy Spirit. Amen.

Day 9

Let us embark on this final day of devotion, invoking the divine presence of the Father, the Son, and the Holy Spirit. Amen.

O most Holy Trinity, Father, Son, and Holy Spirit, we offer our heartfelt praise for the wondrous grace manifested in your servant, St. Clare. Through her powerful intercession, may the favors we seek in this Novena be granted, above all, the grace to lead lives immersed in your holiest love and to find solace in it even in death. Amen.

Gracious St. Clare, who embraced your womanhood with a life dedicated to love, prayer, and penance, assist us in fulfilling our destinies, so that one day we may be welcomed by you in heaven. You, who were comforted at the moment of your passing with a vision of Christ and His Mother, obtain for us the grace to depart from this world under God's special protection, and to enter the luminous and blissful realm you now enjoy. Have compassion on us as we struggle and mourn, and secure for us the blessings of God, so that after this earthly existence, we may return to Him who lives and reigns forever and ever. Amen.

(Share your personal supplications here.)

Pray for us, St. Clare,
   that we may be deemed worthy of Christ's promises.

Lord, we entreat You, grant us, your devoted servants who honor the Feast of St. Clare, your Virgin, to partake in the celestial joys of heaven and become co-heirs with your only begotten Son, who, as God, reigns eternally. Amen.

O glorious St. Clare! God has bestowed upon you the continuous power to work miracles and the gracious favor of answering the prayers of those who seek your assistance in times of misfortune, anxiety, and distress. We earnestly implore you to intercede for us before Jesus, through the blessed intercession of His Mother Mary, so that our fervent and hopeful pleas may be fulfilled, always for the greater glory of God and the betterment of our souls. Amen.

In the name of the Father, the Son, and the Holy Spirit. Amen.

Rosary to Saint Clare of Assisi

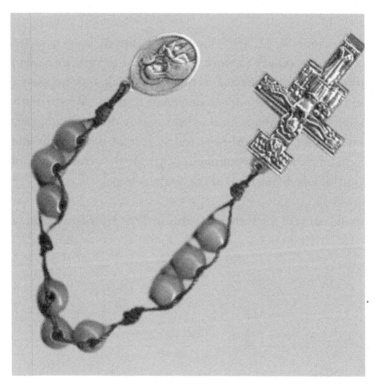

Chaplet of Saint Clare of Assisi

The Chaplet of St. Clare is a devotional prayer that honors and seeks the intercession of Saint Clare of Assisi, a devout follower of St. Francis of Assisi and the foundress of the Poor Clares. The chaplet typically consists of a string of beads or knots and is used by Catholics and other Christians to meditate on and offer prayers to Saint Clare.

The traditional Chaplet of St. Clare is made up of nine beads, symbolizing the nine days of the novena (a period of focused prayer) dedicated to St. Clare. Each day of the novena has a specific theme or intention, and the chaplet helps individuals to focus their prayers and reflections on those themes.

The chaplet begins with an opening prayer, often expressing praise and gratitude to the Holy Trinity and acknowledging the virtues and holiness of St. Clare. It may also ask for her intercession and guidance in following her example of faith, poverty, and love for God.

For each day of the novena, there is a specific prayer or meditation that reflects the particular theme of that day. These themes often highlight different aspects of St. Clare's life, such as her dedication to poverty, her love for the Blessed Sacrament, her trust in God's providence, and her commitment to prayer and penance. Participants are encouraged to offer their personal intentions during each day of the novena.

After the nine days of the novena, the chaplet concludes with a closing prayer, usually asking for St. Clare's continued intercession and the fulfillment of the prayers and intentions offered throughout the novena.

Opening Prayer:

Glorious St. Clare of Assisi, we venerate you for the unwavering faith that led you to forsake earthly delights and relinquish all worldly possessions. We admire your life of profound poverty and austerity, as well as your devoted prayers and penance for the well-being of your fellow nuns and the town of Assisi. Bestow upon us, dear Lady, the same faith, humility, and love that you exemplified towards God and your community. Amen.

Day 1 (Bead One):

Dearest Holy Trinity, Father, Son, and Holy Spirit, we offer our praise and gratitude for the abundant grace that flourished in the life of your humble and gracious servant, Saint Clare. Through her intercession, we humbly approach you like innocent children, seeking not only our heartfelt desires but also the ability to live as Saint Clare did, nestled within Your divine heart. Most Holy Saint Clare, as the first disciple of Saint Francis of Assisi, you willingly abandoned all material riches to embrace a life of sacrifice, service, and poverty, faithfully following the Lord, Our God, through the teachings of the Gospel. Now, in heavenly rejoicing, we implore you to obtain for us from God the grace of (mention your intentions here). We draw inspiration from your profound words, "On earth, may He increase [His] grace and virtues among [His] servants and handmaids of His Church Militant. In heaven, may He exalt and glorify you in His Church Triumphant among all His men and women saints." Most Holy Saint Clare, we aspire to embody the same virtues that graced your life. We strive to become saints like you, dedicated to following the Divine Will and placing our trust in God's providence in every aspect of our existence. Enter our hearts and guide us towards holiness. Saint Clare, intercede for us! That we may be deemed worthy of Christ's promises. Amen.

Day 2 (Bead 2):

Dearest Holy Trinity, Father, Son, and Holy Spirit, we offer our praise and gratitude for the bountiful grace that blossomed in the life of your humble and gracious servant, Saint Clare. Through her intercession, we approach you with childlike innocence, seeking not only our innermost desires but also the ability to mirror Saint Clare's devotion within Your divine heart. Saint Clare, from a tender age, you forsake everything to dedicate your life to God and to serve the poorest of the poor in your hometown of Assisi. Inspired by the words of St. Francis, who directed you towards Jesus and the Most Blessed Sacrament, we implore you to pray for us (mention your intentions here) that we may seek Jesus as our foremost love. Help us grow in love, enabling us to care for the less fortunate and offer our daily lives to God. We draw strength from your words, "The kingdom of heaven is promised and given by the Lord only to the poor: for he who loves temporal things loses the fruit of love." Saint Clare, intercede for us! That we may not seek after worldly possessions but rather seek the love of God! For we understand that material objects cannot fulfill the yearnings of our hearts. Only when our hearts rest in Our Lord, Jesus Christ, will our longings be satisfied. Most Holy Saint Clare, we strive to cultivate poverty of spirit, just as you did. We aspire to become saints like you, devoted to following the Divine Will and placing our trust in God's providence in all aspects of our lives. Enter our hearts and transform us into vessels of holiness. Saint Clare, pray for us! That we may be deserving of Christ's promises. Amen.

Day 3 (Bead 3):

Dearest Holy Trinity, Father, Son, and Holy Spirit, we offer our praise and gratitude for the abundant grace that flourished in the life of your humble and gracious servant, Saint Clare. Through her intercession, we approach you with childlike innocence, seeking not only our heartfelt desires but also the ability to mirror Saint Clare's devotion within Your divine heart. Blessed Saint Clare, whose name signifies "light," illumine the darkness of our minds and hearts, so we may discern God's will for us. Help us joyfully embrace His divine plan. Just as you were a radiant light that illuminated the world, we implore you to be our guiding light during times of difficulty and sorrow. May your brilliance shine so brilliantly that God will swiftly answer the intentions we hold dear in the depths of our hearts (mention your intentions here). Saint Clare, we humbly beseech you to gaze upon our requests with your selfless and compassionate heart. Intercede for us and aid us in our pursuit of holiness! We long for your guidance to lead us towards the eternal light of our heavenly abode. Most Holy Saint Clare, we endeavor to be a beacon of light in the world, just like you. We aspire to become saints like you, dedicated to following the Divine Will and trusting in God's providence in every aspect of our lives. Enter our hearts and sanctify us. Saint Clare, pray for us! That we may be deemed worthy of Christ's promises. Amen.

Day 4 (Bead 4):

Dearest Holy Trinity, Father, Son, and Holy Spirit, we offer our praise and gratitude for the abundant grace that flourished in the life of your humble and gracious servant, Saint Clare. Through her intercession, we approach you with childlike innocence, seeking not only our heartfelt desires but also the ability to mirror Saint Clare's devotion within Your divine heart. Blessed Saint Clare, we draw inspiration from your words, "With swift pace, light step, unswerving feet, so that even your steps stir up no dust, may you go forward securely, joyfully, and swiftly, on the path of prudent happiness, not believing anything that would dissuade you from this resolution or that would place a stumbling block for you on the way, so that you may offer your vows to the Most High in the pursuit of that perfection to which the Spirit of the Lord has called you." Aid us in pursuing the perfection that God intends for us. May we zealously, confidently, and joyfully pursue the Lord every day of our lives, regardless of our vocation, whether religious, married, or single. Assist us in finding happiness both in our lives and in God, the Most High. With great confidence, we seek your intercession for (mention your intentions here). We firmly believe in your ability to present our requests directly to the Lord, and we trust that He will hear and answer us, for you are a powerful intercessor. Most Holy Saint Clare, we aspire to find happiness in our lives as you did. We strive to become saints like you, dedicated to following the Divine Will and trusting in God's providence in every aspect of our lives. Enter our hearts and sanctify us. Saint Clare, pray for us! That we may be deserving of Christ's promises. Amen.

Day 5 (Bead 5):

Dearest Holy Trinity, Father, Son, and Holy Spirit, we offer our praise and gratitude for the abundant grace that flourished in the life of your humble and gracious servant, Saint Clare. Through her intercession, we approach you with childlike innocence, seeking not only our heartfelt desires but also the ability to mirror Saint Clare's devotion within Your divine heart. Blessed Saint Clare, we are deeply moved by your words, "Place your mind in the mirror of eternity; Place your soul in the splendor of glory; Place your heart in the figure of the divine substance; And, through contemplation, transform your entire being into the image of the Divine One Himself; So that you, yourself, may also experience what His friends experience when they taste the hidden sweetness that God alone has kept from the beginning. For those who love Him." Assist us in surrendering our minds, souls, and hearts to the care of the Lord. Guide us in contemplation and the transformation of our entire beings into devoted followers of God. Glorious Saint Clare, you lived a life marked by love, prayer, and penance. Aid us in fulfilling our destinies, so that one day we may join you in Heaven. We implore you, compassionate Saint Clare, to have mercy on us as we grapple with our faith. Your faith is unwavering, and thus we confidently seek your intercession (mention your intentions here), that we may also savor the sweetness that God reserves for those who love Him. Most Holy Saint Clare, we endeavor to be faithful, just like you. We aspire to become saints like you, dedicated to following the Divine Will and trusting in God's providence in every aspect of our lives. Enter our hearts and sanctify us. Saint Clare, pray for us! That we may be deserving of Christ's promises. Amen.

Day 6 (Bead 6):

Dearest Holy Trinity, Father, Son, and Holy Spirit, we offer our praise and gratitude for the abundant grace that flourished in the life of your humble and gracious servant, Saint Clare. Through her intercession, we approach you with childlike innocence, seeking not only our heartfelt desires but also the ability to mirror Saint Clare's devotion within Your divine heart. Blessed Saint Clare, we find inspiration in your words, "May He look upon you with the eyes of His mercy and give you His peace. Here below may He pour forth His graces on you abundantly and in Heaven may He place you among His saints." Aid us in embracing the Lord's gaze so that we may find true peace. May His mercy dissolve all anxiety, distress, and hardships, for we yearn to rest peacefully in God's plan for our lives. You lived a contemplative life of prayer, silence, and peace. In this bustling and noisy world, bestow upon us your wisdom and tranquil nature, so that we may better hear God's voice. With unwavering desire and faith, we bring our intentions (mention your intentions here) peacefully to your feet, knowing that you will promptly present our prayers before the Lord, Our God. Most Holy Saint Clare, we aspire to embody peace, just like you. We strive to become saints like you, devoted to following the Divine Will and trusting in God's providence in every aspect of our lives. Enter our hearts and sanctify us. Saint Clare, pray for us! That we may be deserving of Christ's promises. Amen.

Day 7 (Bead 7):

Dearest Holy Trinity, Father, Son, and Holy Spirit, we offer our praise and gratitude for the abundant grace that flourished in the life of your humble and gracious servant, Saint Clare. Through her intercession, we approach you with childlike innocence, seeking not only our heartfelt desires but also the ability to mirror Saint Clare's devotion within Your divine heart. Blessed Saint Clare, we find inspiration in your words, "Go forth without fear, for He who created you has made you holy, has always protected you, and loves you as a mother. Blessed be you, my God, for having created me." Aid us in becoming fearless like you, O Saint Clare. Your unwavering trust in God and the Blessed Sacrament as your protection encourages us to follow in your faithful footsteps. When your convent faced an impending attack, you fearlessly placed the Eucharist at the gates, prayed fervently, and your attackers retreated. Show us how to be fearless in our faith, just as you were, so that we may not be intimidated by the sufferings in our world today but rather overcome them with triumphant courage. Glorious Saint Clare, from your elevated place in Heaven, watch over us now and attend to our needs (mention your intentions here), guiding us with your illuminating light toward Heaven. Most Holy Saint Clare, we endeavor to be fearless like you. We strive to become saints like you, devoted to following the Divine Will and trusting in God's providence in every aspect of our lives. Enter our hearts and sanctify us. Saint Clare, pray for us! That we may be deserving of Christ's promises. Amen.

Day 8 (Bead 8):

Dearest Holy Trinity, Father, Son, and Holy Spirit, we offer our praises for the abundant grace that blossomed in the life of your humble and gracious servant, Saint Clare. Through her intercession, we approach you with childlike simplicity, seeking not only our heartfelt petitions but also the grace to emulate Saint Clare's love within Your divine heart. Blessed Saint Clare, we find inspiration in your words, "Love with your whole heart God and Jesus, His son, crucified for our sins, and never let His memory escape your mind; make yourself meditate continually on the mysteries of the cross and the anguish of the mother standing beneath the cross." Aid us in loving God and Jesus as you did. May we always remember the profound sacrifice He made out of love for us. Your love for God led you to offer your life to Him under the guidance of St. Francis. Be our guide! Show us how to love God and every person we encounter, just as you passionately loved God and selflessly served the poor. With unwavering faith in you, O Saint Clare, we implore you to intercede for us (mention your intentions here). Beloved by God and close to His heart, please do not overlook our requests but lovingly present them before God for His consideration. Most Holy Saint Clare, we strive to be filled with love like you. We endeavor to become saints like you, faithfully following the Divine Will and entrusting ourselves to God's providence in all aspects of our lives. Enter our hearts and sanctify us. Saint Clare, pray for us! That we may be deserving of Christ's promises. Amen.

Day 9 (Bead 9):

Dearest Holy Trinity, Father, Son, and Holy Spirit, we offer our praises for the abundant grace that blossomed in the life of your humble and gracious servant, Saint Clare. Through her intercession, we approach you with childlike simplicity, seeking not only our heartfelt petitions but also the grace to emulate Saint Clare's love within Your divine heart. Most prayerful Saint Clare, we admire the example you set for your sisters and for everyone in the world. You remained a faithful daughter of the Church and a trusted companion of popes, cardinals, bishops, and many holy individuals. Illuminate us with your prayerful words, "I, Clare, a handmaid of Christ, a little plant of our holy Father Francis, a sister and mother to you and the Poor Sisters, although unworthy, ask our Lord Jesus Christ, through His mercy and the intercession of His most holy Mother Mary, Blessed Michael the Archangel, all the holy angels of God, and all His men and women saints, to bestow and confirm upon you this most holy blessing in heaven and on earth." With your prayer, O Blessed Saint Clare, we entreat you to bring our intentions to the Most High God in Heaven (mention your intentions here). Our Father, as we celebrate the feast of Saint Clare, we pray that you may grant us to partake in the joys of Heaven. Most Holy Saint Clare, we strive to be prayerful like you. We endeavor to become saints like you, faithfully following the Divine Will and entrusting ourselves to God's providence in all aspects of our lives. Enter our hearts and sanctify us. Saint Clare, pray for us! That we may be deserving of Christ's promises. Amen.

Closing Prayer:

O glorious Saint Clare! God has bestowed upon you the power of working miracles continually, and the favor of answering the prayers of those who seek your assistance in times of misfortune, anxiety, and distress. We humbly beseech you, obtain for us from Jesus, through Mary, His Blessed Mother, the fervent and hopeful requests we bring before you, if it be for the greater honor and glory of God and for the well-being of our souls. Saint Clare, pray for us. Amen.

Other Prayers Offered to St. Clare

Prayer to St. Clare of Assisi

Oh blessed Saint Clare of Assisi, I come to you with faith and love in my heart, adorned with the desire for your intercession. Please help me present my intention to the Lord and help me trust that it will be answered. I adore your devotion to God and see myself learning from how greatly you placed Him as Your Master and Lover. Intercede for us all so that we may always experience His peace. Amen.

Prayer to St. Clare for Good Weather

O glorious St. Clare, intercede with our Lord and Savior, Jesus Christ, for us in prayer. We humbly ask that you use your divine power to bring peace and comfort to those who suffer from unstable weather conditions. Grant us sunny skies and gentle breezes so that all may benefit from the beauty of nature's gifts. Please grant us favorable temperatures; let the sun warm our faces, but not too hot or too cool. Help keep harsh windstorms at bay and severe rain away from our homes, businesses, and communities. Let your prayers fill our skies with beautiful sunshine! Amen!

Prayer to St. Clare for Healing

O Lord, I humbly implore Your grace and mercy as I turn to St. Clare for her intercession in healing my ailing body and broken spirit. As she stood before You in awe-filled adoration of the Eucharistic Presence, so too do I kneel before You with a heart open to receive Your transformative power. Grant me the strength to remain humble and hopeful even when affliction strikes me. Through her trials, Saint Clare remained steadfast in her trust that You would restore peace to those who called upon You, I pray for the same faith. Let your Blessed Mother Mary be my ally as I face these challenges; may Saint Clare find favor with you on my behalf! Amen.

Prayer to St. Clare for Baby

Oh, Glorious Saint Clare, you shared in the life of St. Francis and were a devoted follower of his teachings. I turn to you with warm feelings as I ask for your intercession on behalf of my baby, who needs your help and protection. Please guide this little one so that they remain safe and healthy, their souls overflowing with joy and peace. I ask that you keep every harm away from them as they sleep so that each day brings them closer to God's love. Amen.

Prayer to St. Clare for Eyes

O Blessed Saint Clare, I come before Your Divine presence with a heavy heart full of distress. I seek You out in my need and loneliness to help me see again with clarity and focus. Grant me the gift of sight once more, for it is to You that I entrust the wellbeing of my eyes. Through binding them up where gratitude will open them, may I learn to appreciate every detail existence has to offer and behold joyful visions of eternity in The Most Blessed Sacrament. Give me strength through Your loving grace so that Your blessings may be found ceaselessly within my life, offering comfort even in affliction or darkness, as You have done throughout Your lifetime. Amen.

Made in the USA
Las Vegas, NV
18 March 2024

A Dictionary *of*
——— Modern ———
Star Names
A Short Guide to 254 Star Names and Their Derivations